BECOMING A BETTER BOSS

Your Guidebook to 25 Fundamental Management Responsibilities

This is written for leaders, managers, and supervisors everywhere who are dedicated to bringing out the best in the people they serve.

HERE'S TO YOUR FUTURE!

Lorna Kibbey

ISBN-13: 978-1724279187

ISBN-10: 1724279181

For permission requests, contact the author at the address below.

Lorna Kibbey Leadership Solutions

Fort Myers, FL USA

LKibbey@LKibbey.com

www.LKibbey.com

Printed in the United States of America

Although the author has made every effort to ensure that the information in this book was correct at press time, the author does not assume a███████aim any liability to any party for any███████sruption caused by errors or omissions, whether such errors or omissions result from negligence, accident, or any other cause. The information provided is intended to serve as quick guides to help with fundamental, yet critical, leadership tasks.

BECOMING A BETTER BOSS

TABLE OF CONTENTS

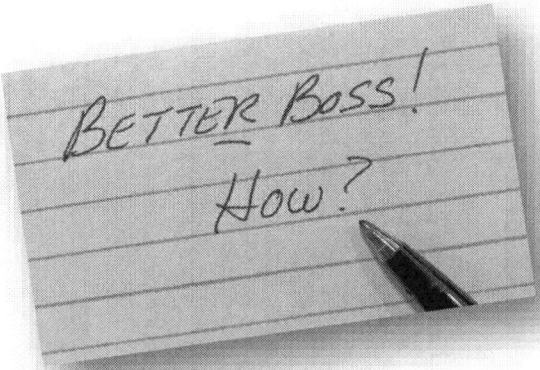

PREFACE

This book is intended to be a reference book. Included are 25 guides for responsibilities that bosses continuously juggle. The guides are in themselves lessons on how to handle responsibilities and situations that are known to be important, and often difficult.

If you are a new boss, you need this book. Having guides to all of these tasks in one place will make it easy for you to take a quick look to ensure you are on track, and to understand how to dig deeper if needed.

If you are an experienced boss, you need this book. Use these guides as checklists to ensure you are being the best boss, ever!

While you may want to read this book cover-to-cover, it is okay to read the chapters out of order. You should feel free to highlight what is important to you and mark sections that you will want to find quickly. And, you will find overlap as the job of the boss cannot be divided into 25 little packages all independent of one another.

What I find interesting is that the subjects in themselves are commonly known and there are assumptions that we just know how to do these things. Yet, when training and coaching bosses these are the very subjects they request help with, over and over.

I can say with confidence: the topics have been chosen by demand — the demand of all bosses who struggle with these common responsibilities and ask for help in managing them.

Enjoy.

INTRODUCTION

Becoming a better boss begins with a simple formula.

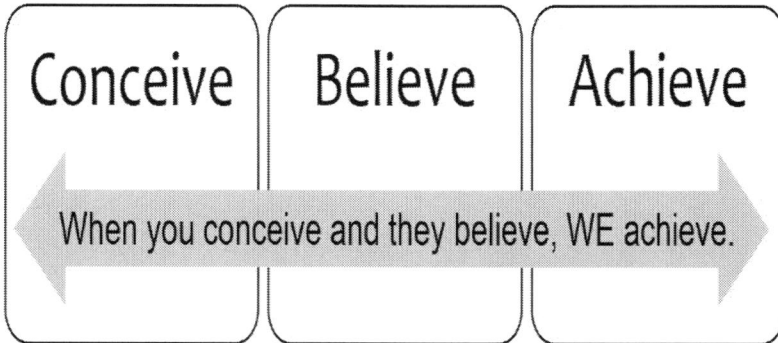

Conceive	Believe	Achieve
When you conceive and they believe, WE achieve.		

If you are a boss, you are most likely looking for ways to be a better boss, to bring out the best in employees, to connect with each person, to include, engage, and encourage them. There are specific things a boss can do to develop people into trustworthy, high performing, and happy employees.

Conceive

The boss must first define the vision, goals, expectations, and priorities for his or her team. In order for people to do great work, they need to understand what is expected of them!

Work with staff to help them develop goals that will get you where you need to go. When you involve your employees in this process they will:

- Better understand the purpose of their work.
- Have an opportunity to be creative.
- Have input and feel included.
- Build trust.

Although many of the guides in this book indirectly provide help with this concept, specific guidance is included in:

- Change
- Communication
- Developing a Supervisory Mindset
- E-mail Writing
- Leader or Manager
- Presentations
- Priorities
- Setting Expectations
- Vision

Believe

People want to do meaningful work. They need to understand how their work contributes to the big picture.

People need an opportunity to buy-in on both emotional and task levels. They need to understand "why."

The boss must ensure alignment – that everyone is going in the same direction. Education must be provided continuously, and commitment is critical to success.

When you involve your employees in this process you will:
- Build trust.
- Engage employees.
- Build independence.
- Help employees advance.
- Build commitment.
- Show employees they are valued and respected.

Again, many of the guides in this book indirectly provide help with this concept. Specific guidance is included in:
- Coaching, Counseling, and Mentoring
- Conflict
- Consensus
- Developing Employee Talent
- Empowering Employees
- Meetings with Staff
- Meeting with Employees One-on-One
- Personalities
- Teamwork

Achieve

For all organizations, achievement of results is the ultimate goal. The boss must ensure there is a structured plan, be willing to give and receive feedback, and keep momentum high. Recognizing desired performance – celebration – is a vital part of achievement.

When you involve your employees in this process they will:

- Feel appreciated
- Build confidence
- Be happier
- Advance in their careers

Again, many of the guides in this book indirectly provide help with this concept. Specific guidance is included in:

➢ Appreciation
➢ Delegation
➢ Feedback
➢ Momentum
➢ Motivation
➢ Performance Appraisal
➢ Time Management

If you are an experienced leader, take some time to think about your performance as a boss, in each of these three areas. If you are new to leadership, know that each of these three areas have specific steps you can take to become a better boss.

The guides in this book interweave and will empower you to be that Better Boss!

1. APPRECIATION

Celebration is an important task for any leader. It is also one that often gets pushed to the side – who has the time to have a party? This is not about having a party – it is about expressing appreciation to your employees for the work they do. Everyone needs to feel appreciated. Here are simple tips that won't take much time.

FOR INDIVIDUALS – FOCUS ON PRAISE

Praise is one of the easiest rewards you can give and it is a motivator for everyone when done right. By simply pointing out something that someone did and letting them know you appreciated it, you are reinforcing behavior that you want to see again. By recognizing desired performance, you teach what you value, and what is important.

Remember to praise:

- *Specifically:* praise people for specific accomplishments.

- *Spontaneously:* catch people doing something right and thank them then and there.

- *Purposefully:* take an employee to lunch or dinner.

- *Privately:* give a personal thank you and praise.

- *Publicly:* praise an employee in the presence of others.

- *In writing:* send a letter, memo, or e-mail. Possibly send a copy to a team member's higher-level manager!

FOR TEAMS – FOCUS ON ACCOMPLISHMENTS

- Identify the major *accomplishments of the team* over a specific time period.

- Have each team member discuss their *personal experience* in working with the team.

- Ask team members to *acknowledge their teammates* who made contributions.

- Find ways to accentuate and advertise your team's positive results, every day!

- Throw a party! Order a cake, plan a luncheon, organize a fun event and show appreciation to the whole team.

FOR ALL – A NOTE ABOUT REWARDS

It's best that a supervisor has an inventory of different types of rewards. Remember these important rules:

1. If an employee expects it, it may no longer be viewed as a reward.
2. Rewards need to match your employee's needs and wants. Many managers wrongly assume that every employee likes or wants the same kinds of rewards and recognition.
3. After you put your employee reward system into place, you need to check periodically to ensure it is producing the results intended. If it isn't, you need to change it.
4. The best reward – no question – is specific targeted appreciation. "You did a great job in facilitating that meeting! You politely kept people on task, on subject, and ended on time. Nice work."

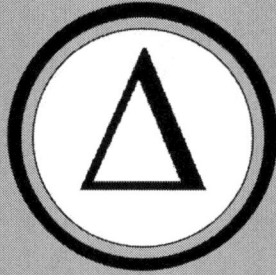

2. CHANGE

Things change so rapidly that change has become normal, expected, and for some – desired. It's almost surprising that we still need to talk about change management with the world as it is today. For many, change is not easy and is spite of everything, it's easy to understand why.

We know that people in general, want to be good at what they do. They want to master their work and their work environment. Such mastery gives one the feeling of being in control. When change occurs, we feel threatened. It's natural. Problem is, change is also natural. As Benjamin Franklin so wisely stated in the 1700's:

"When we're finished changing, we're finished."

Yikes.

SO WHAT CAN LEADERS DO?

Leaders must first work to understand change. We often downplay some of the most basic concepts of change. Many people in leadership roles are not threatened by change. They sometimes have difficulty assessing the intensity of the impact at ground level. They are looking at a much bigger picture.

What are they leaving out of the equation? Probably the biggest factor is that change – no matter how small – takes time to implement. Just making a change and saying so, doesn't make it so. If employees haven't bought in, you might get compliance but little more. Change experts agree that employees go through five stages as they make the transition – much like the five stages of grief!

1. SHOCK is first. Denial happens here. People are shocked that this change is happening. They are shocked that by the method that will be employed, shocked by the way it was announced, and so on.

2. EMOTION is next – usually anger. Once the shock wears off, people get upset – sometimes angry, sometimes tearful, and need to express their feelings.

3. BARGAINING follows. Maybe the change doesn't have to be as radical as announced? Employees begin to question: "Maybe we could just do part of it? Maybe we could work harder to make the old way work? Maybe I should look for another job?" What they are expressing is, "Hey, let's talk about this first."

4. DEPRESSION accompanies all change. It's really a grieving process. Even when change is good there is a natural pause. We naturally have feelings of loss and we grieve these losses no matter how insignificant they may seem.

5. ACCEPTANCE finally comes. This occurs when people have come to understand the change on an intellectual and emotional level. Only then can they move on.

This process cannot be charted out on a timeline. Experts tell us that it takes 1 to 1 ½ years to work through these five stages – and that doesn't mean 2 to 4 months each. Every person moves through the phases at their own rate. For example, Phase 1 – Shock, may last 24 hours while Phase 2 – Emotion, lasts for months. It is possible for a person to get stuck in any one of these stages. Moving on may be extremely difficult, or even impossible.

Bottom line, acceptance of change will not be immediate. It takes time. We must be aware of the stages of change and provide support. Otherwise, employees with best intentions will begin to resent what is happening. They may become emotionally or physically ill. They may become "difficult." Burnout and turnover may occur.

WHAT LEADERS MUST KNOW

Change produces fear.

Perception is distorted during times of change – you'll need to increase communication.

If you don't regularly share information, people will make up their own. Some call it gossip.

Honesty is a necessity.

People need stability – change is best in small chunks. Keep things as familiar as you can.

Grieving is normal and necessary.

Dealing with change is stressful – help employees take care of themselves.

Taking time to meet as a team for the purpose of doing something fun, is a must! They need opportunities to be with others and share stories, experiences, and good news.

3. COACHING, COUNSELING, AND MENTORING

Which to Use and When

We need to constantly encourage and guide our employees – the question is what is the right way to do what and when! Coaching, counseling, and mentoring are techniques used daily by bosses everywhere, and all three have specific purposes. Let's discuss the differences and benefits of each.

COACHING

COACH Something or someone who carries a valued person from where they are to where they want to be.	You might be interested to know this definition originates from the 15th century. "Coaches" were first built in Kocs, Hungary to carry royalty over bumpy roads!

Coaching focuses on positive reinforcement and development of new skills.

- Coaching *IS* a conversation focused on helping others move forward.
- Coaching *IS NOT* about giving advice. (That's mentoring!)
- Coaching *IS* tied to something the person wants to accomplish – the goals *they* want to achieve.
- Coaching *IS NOT* about therapeutic outcomes.
- Coaching *IS* about making improvements in individual and organizational performance.

When Coaching . . .

- Learn to question – instead of tell.
- Be aware of differences in style.
- Plan questions in advance.
- Start where they are – instead of where you think they should be.
- Check understanding frequently.
- Talk 20% of the time, listen 80% of the time.

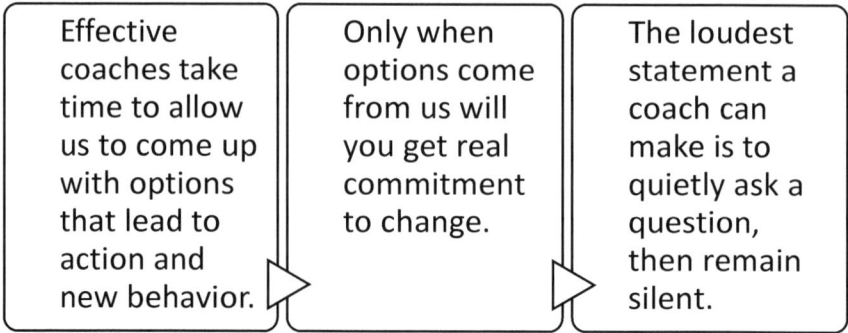

Effective coaches take time to allow us to come up with options that lead to action and new behavior.	Only when options come from us will you get real commitment to change.	The loudest statement a coach can make is to quietly ask a question, then remain silent.

MENTORING

MENTOR	YOUR MENTORS
A wise and trusted teacher or counselor.	Who has mentored you?

A Coach and a Mentor have different job. While a coach helps an employee to learn new skills, to reinforce positive behavior, and to achieve the next performance level; a mentor focuses more on support and development.

COACH	MENTOR
▪ Someone who is there FOR you.	▪ Someone who was there BEFORE you.
▪ Someone who knows how to ask the right questions.	▪ Someone who can support you based on their experience.
▪ Task oriented and performance driven.	▪ Relationship oriented and development driven.

Mentoring can be done formally or informally. Often, mentoring relationships are informal – sometimes even accidental! If you are considering a mentoring program for your employees, consider putting together a more formal effort.

Either way, here are basic steps for getting started. Know that mentoring relationships require commitment from both parties to achieve successful outcomes.

To get started with mentoring:

- ☐ Find a mentor/protégé (don't be afraid to ask).
- ☐ Establish relationship rules (how do you want to be contacted, for example).
- ☐ Agree on a schedule for meetings.
- ☐ Begin with the end in mind. (Goals!)
- ☐ Write a "contract" and define expectations on both sides of the relationship.

COUNSELING

COUNSEL	
Formal advice given in directing behavior or conduct of another.	COUNSELING is used to focus on corrective action, to change inappropriate or undesired behavior.

Counseling is used to focus on corrective action and changing inappropriate or ineffective behavior.

What is counseling?

- Guidance
- Something to provide direction
- A means of assisting and developing
- A way to address specific behavior patterns
- Exploring and finding options to help facilitate change

If you are at the point of counseling an employee, it is most likely time to involve your support systems (such as Human Resources or your boss). By definition, counseling is needed when the goal is to change undesired behavior.

To get started, know that correctively counseling generally includes some form of these four steps:

1. **Assessing – What is the problem?**
    1. Why is the behavior undesirable?
    2. Are co-workers feeling the impact?
    3. What's your theory?
    4. Is there an easy fix?
    5. What action is needed to solve this?
    6. Is this a performance or disciplinary issue?

2. **Meeting – Discuss the situation with the employee.**
    - ☐ Logistics – Where? When? Who should be present?
    - ☐ Face-to-Face – Take time to listen and consider their point of view.
    - ☐ Action – Agree on specific action to be taken.

3. **Documenting – Keep a record of the facts.**
    - ☐ Record FACTS, not opinion.
    - ☐ Be specific!
    - ☐ Include details.
    - ☐ Remember to use all available sources of documentation. (For example: time sheets, notes,

work samples, Email messages, and many other sources that are in your work environment.)

4. **Following Through – See it through to resolution.**
   - ☐ Monitor your action plan and their performance.
   - ☐ Document using a performance diary or other tool.
   - ☐ Track – use your calendar to stay on track.
   - ☐ Communicate – make positive comments to the employee to show you are monitoring.
   - ☐ Meeting with the employee to coach!

One last point, if things do not progress in spite of your efforts, do not procrastinate. Move on to the next step. Allowing the situation to go on will seriously impact the performance of your entire team.

___

In summary, there are distinct differences in coaching, counseling and mentoring. It is wise to understand the differences and be able to use the best technique to get desired results.

Coaching is used to help an employee learn new skills, to reinforce positive behavior, to reach the next level.

Mentoring focuses on support and development.

Counseling is used to change inappropriate or undesired behavior.

"I've learned that people will forget what you said, people will forget what you did, but people will never forget how you made them feel."

-Maya Angelou

4. COMMUNICATION
STRUCTURED MESSAGING

Many leaders have the ability to speak extemporaneously. They don't find it necessary to spend time preparing what they will say as they can form the message in their minds and deliver it on demand.

Though this ability may exist, there are problems caused by this type of communication. Unstructured messages result when a leader communicates with a group without thinking through three critical elements:

1. The order of the message.
2. What questions the audience will want answered?
3. What outcome the leader expects as a result of the message.

Many times, a leader delivers what they believe to be the same message to different audiences – or to the same audience at different times – not understanding that they presented the message differently in some small way. What often results is confusion and frustration – and sometimes, gossip.

If you have any doubts about the importance of delivering a consistent message every time, with every audience, every individual, every day – just answer this question: What is the most prevalent problem in almost every organization? Indeed, communication is the answer.

Taking time to structure your message up front is not time consuming. In fact, time will be saved in the long run. Simply start with an index card and write down:

1. Your purpose
2. Your talking points
3. What should happen next – action item!

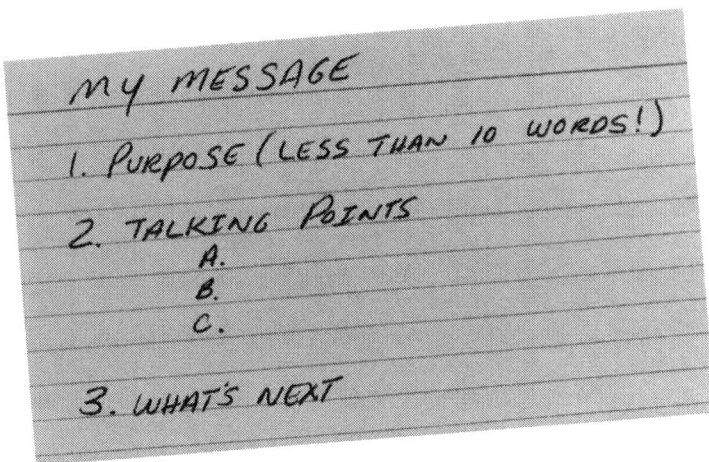

MY MESSAGE
1. PURPOSE (LESS THAN 10 WORDS!)
2. TALKING POINTS
   A.
   B.
   C.

3. WHAT'S NEXT

Now that you have a structured message, here are tips for maximizing effectiveness.

☐ Look at the order of your talking points. Consider what questions your audience will have. Rearrange if necessary to make sure information is presented in a manner that is logical to your audience.

☐ Use your index card to "redundantly" communicate – in other words, to repeat the message the same way at different times, to different audience, through different mediums. For example, after preparing your index card, use it to write an Email. Then use it again when you verbally deliver the message. If you have a one-on-one with an employee, again refer to the index card to be sure you are presenting the message the same way every time. This will result in consistent messages and clear communication.

☐ Continue referring back to your index card – don't rely on your memory – or your "gut."

Taking the time to structure your message, and think it through before delivery, results in clarity. It will help you to deliver relevant information effectively, leave out details your audience doesn't need to hear again, and ensure everyone hears the message as intended.

5. CONFLICT

Productive conflict is required for an organization to grow. Teams that engage in healthy conflict have lively meetings using ideas of all team members. They solve problems quickly and discuss critical topics. Team members who share conflict may use that energy to create a surprising solution to a problem. Conflict isn't all bad – still we must find ways to manage conflict before it becomes destructive.

Let's be clear, there are different types of conflict a boss must handle. Sometimes, conflict exists between two people, employees who just don't get along. Other times, conflict erupts when a group of employees work together to solve a problem. Conflict is all around us. The first step is to understand the value of conflict and adjust your thinking so you can use it wisely.

To get in the right frame of mind, let's think about the concept of debate. A debate is a structured argument. Two sides take turns speaking for and against a particular issue. Each person or team is given an equal amount of time to state their case.

Debate is something we have used for hundreds of years to formally discuss disagreements. Our schools have debate clubs and team competitions. Students of debate have a chance to prove a point and have their reasoning tested. Our society values differences of opinion.

So why is it that in some settings debate is celebrated and encouraged and in office settings it is often considered a "conflict?"

The best way for a boss to address conflict is to address it before it is considered a conflict. How?

BETWEEN EMPLOYEES

Frequently and openly discuss how problems should be solved by employees.

- Teach employees how healthfully debate.

- Encourage people to openly discuss issues.

- Give opportunities for employees to learn their personal style in conflict situations.

- Reach agreement on when people in conflict should ask for intervention.

PERSONAL CONFLICT RESOLUTION TIPS

When in a conflict situation, here are some things to consider.

- First assess the situation. Are you helping or hurting?

- Try to resolve. Have an open discussion and seek common ground.

- Use "I" language. (Example: "I feel like you think I am to blame." versus "You always blame me.")

- Avoid insulting language such as "You always . . ."

- Watch your tone of voice.

- Learn to listen empathetically.

- Know your "anger buttons" and don't let them be pushed.

MANAGEMENT INTERVENTION TIPS

When conflict between employees reaches a level that requires management intervention, it is best not to ignore it or hope it gets better on its own.

1. Listen! There are two sides to every story and they need to tell you as much as you need to listen.

2. Focus on facts, but don't ignore feelings. If they need your intervention, they need to "clear the air."

3. Take charge. Help them see the bigger picture and possible implications of their conflict.

THE TEAM

As the boss, you will need to give your team permission to openly debate issues during meetings.

- Establish trust on your work team by meeting regularly. Help employees get to know each other.

- Teach your team the difference between healthy debate and destructive conflict.

- Do not shy away from healthy debate in team meetings. Allow people to disagree.

- Be a good facilitator. Watch for the point where debate is turning away from productive. Immediately stop, summarize progress, and move on.

DESTRUCTIVE CONFLICT WARNING SIGNS
➢ Finger-pointing
➢ Ultimatums
➢ Insults
➢ Defensiveness
➢ Avoidance
➢ Threats
➢ Shut-down
➢ Disregard of facts

Empathetic Listening

Empathetic listening – or active listening, must be practiced. As the boss, constantly remind yourself:

- Listen as if you need to repeat back what they said.

- Listen for words that are not spoken.

- Acknowledge their feelings.

- Spend more time listening than talking.

- Do something about what you hear.

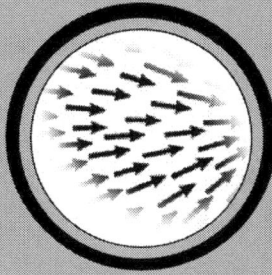

6. CONSENSUS

Consensus

Everyone agrees to support a team decision.

Consensus does not mean everyone agrees with a particular decision. That will rarely happen. It means they agree that of all options, the decision made is the best choice.

Our goal is for everyone to leave a meeting and openly, willingly, and publicly support the decision made. To achieve that goal, the team leader will need to "test" consensus.

The reason to test consensus is to ensure that everyone present has the chance to express their opinion and ask their questions. Each person must have the opportunity to influence the decision of the group.

Some leaders "test" consensus by asking the standard question: "Does everyone agree?" That question usually gets head nods – or indifferent stares. To leave the meeting with a true consensus, that is not enough. If that is as far as you go to get consensus, you run the risk of having at least one person who does not agree or support the decision. How can we expect to succeed if every single team member isn't "all in" on decisions made?

The process steps for testing consensus include:

1. *Identify All Options*

   First, list all options. If possible, start with brainstorming so that everyone can get ideas out there. Record all ideas so that people can see them "on paper." (Use a flip chart, a white board, PowerPoint, or similar tool to list the ideas as they are shared.)

2. *Build on Common Ideas*

   The work of brainstorming together allows your team to build on ideas as they arise. Continue to explore until the group feels they have a complete list of ideas and options.

3. *Propose Alternatives or Compromises*

   Now it's time to narrow the list and look at possible alternatives. Consider researching best ways to help participants vote anonymously on top choices. (Tip: Nominal Group Technique is a great method for group decision making.)

4. *Discuss Differences*

Now that the list of ideas has been shortened, allow participants to discuss the options. Try going down your list and having participants shout out pros and cons of each idea.

5. *Identify Best Choices*

Identify the best choices and work with the group to narrow your list to the top two or three. If necessary, do another round of anonymous voting to narrow the list even more and to ultimately identify the number one choice.

6. *Test Consensus*

The final step is to ask each participant in turn, "Will you support this decision?" It is important to ask one person at a time. Watch their non-verbal response as you listen for the verbal response. If there is any doubt in their response, stop and ask what's bothering them. Each person needs a chance to weigh in. Remember, they can't buy in unless they have the opportunity to weigh in!

"It's as simple as this. When people don't unload their opinions and feel like they've been listened to, they won't really get on board."

- Patrick Lencioni

"The Five Dysfunctions of a Team: A Leadership Fable"

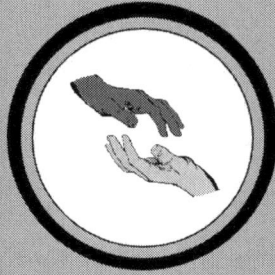

7. DELEGATION
THE RIGHT WAY

Delegation

The assignment of responsibilities to others, along with the authority and resources needed to complete a job.

We all understand the importance of delegation. Delegation increases a supervisor's productivity. The organization gains strength as others become educated in the work of the team. Job satisfaction and engagement increase as employees are given a variety of assignments and new learning opportunities.

All good! So why do managers resist delegating? Managers worry about getting the job done right.

It is often faster to do a task yourself than to teach someone else. And how can you justify giving your employee yet another task? You, as the manager, are accountable, so all in all, it is easier to just do it yourself.

On the other side, your employees are fearful. Fearful of failing, becoming overloaded, and of being micromanaged. Yet, retention studies repeatedly show that employees crave growth and challenge. They need opportunities to use their skills in new ways and to expand their knowledge.

We know the benefits of delegation far outweigh the drawbacks. The good news is that delegation works – when it is done the right way!

Here are Five Steps of Delegation. These five steps will guide you through and when followed, ensure the job will be done right.

Caution! Caution! Caution!

- Know that your employee will not perform the task exactly as you would. Be patient, focus on outcomes, and see this as an opportunity to look at different ways of accomplishing work.
- Some tasks should not be delegated such as disciplinary duties, confidential situations, performance feedback, and other personal assignments that you must handle.

FIVE STEPS OF DELEGATION

STEP 1 – Analyze the Task

First you need to analyze the task and clearly define what a successful outcome will be. Remember, if your employee isn't clear on your vision and expectations for this task, it is likely he/she will put wasted effort in to working on the wrong things.

Questions to answer as you analyze the task:

1. What is the task?
2. When is it due?
3. Why does it need to be done?
4. What complications may arise?
5. What resources are available?
6. What is the desired outcome or deliverable?

STEP 2 – Select the Right Employee

People have different strengths and different levels of experience. You will need to carefully choose the right person for the job. Consider what your employee may need and determine his or her level of readiness.

Delegation is a powerful learning tool – you will not always delegate to the most competent and committed employee.

Three steps to follow:

> Identify skills and attitude needed.

> Match needed skills to employees.

> Arrange for any necessary training.

STEP 3 – Assign the Task and Empower Your Employee

Questions you would expect to answer as you assign the task.

1. What is the task's goal or expected outcome?

2. What actions, assistance, or resources will be required?

3. When is it due?

4. When and how will we follow up?

5. How will it affect their workload?

6. What obstacles does the employee foresee?

7. What authority does the employee have?

8. What are the benefits and consequences of the task?

STEP 4 – Execute, Step Back, and Let Go!

1. Review agreements made during task assignment.

2. Set up a regular schedule of meetings with the employee to check progress.

3. Review the authority that your employee has been given with the assignment and inform those impacted.

4. Allow the employee to get to work! (Tip: Do not micromanage!)

STEP 5 – Track Progress and Provide Support

Monitoring progress is critical in delegation. It can be done differently depending on the person and the task. To effectively monitor, a boss must:

- Keep communication open.
- Set reminders to check-in with the employee.
- Follow through on benchmarks and expectations.
- Praise for good progress and redirect when needed.
- Give feedback regularly.

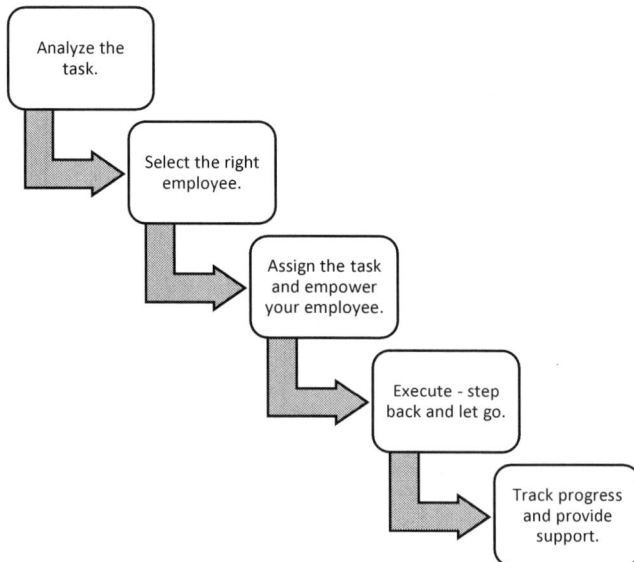

Analyze the task.

Select the right employee.

Assign the task and empower your employee.

Execute - step back and let go.

Track progress and provide support.

GETTING STARTED WITH DELEGATION

If you are still living in fear of delegating, start small.

- Delegate tasks that won't have a significant impact if something goes wrong.

- Carefully assess the level of the employee's expertise. Assign tasks that meet or slightly exceed their level.

- Set schedules for follow-up.

- Monitor performance.

- Don't forget to praise – and redirect when needed!

If you are worried about an employee's ability to handle delegated tasks, try this:

1. Ask them to be fact finders only. Give them a research project and have them bring you their findings. Discuss with them how well they did – were they thorough? Did they focus on the right thing?

2. Next ask them to use their findings to make suggestions for solving a problem. How did they do?

3. Now that you are more confident in their abilities, ask them to implement one of their recommendations – with your approval.

4. Next step – have them take action and then report the results to you right away.

5. Finally, give them complete authority using the steps of delegation described.

8. DEVELOPING EMPLOYEE TALENT

People need opportunities to grow and learn. Read any available retention survey and you will see this is true across industries, generations, and experience levels.

As a leader, knowing that your employees need to grow and learn is essential. Basic motivation theory tells us that when a need is present, we will search for ways to meet that need. If you as my leader want me to perform better for our organization, you will need to guide me in finding the right learning opportunities. Create an environment that encourages and supports my need to learn more and grow.

There are many opportunities for those who want to be continuous learners. No shortage exists in ways to expand personal knowledge. Often, employees will seek out information on their own. Problem is, the information they find may not be correct – or even relevant – to your organization.

Here are ideas for providing development opportunities that will keep employees on the right track in developing relevant and needed skills and behaviors. Remember, the leader must be supportive and involved in these efforts.

Video Case Study

Assign employees the task of bringing one video of less than five minutes, to designated staff meetings. The employee is tasked with choosing a video they feel would help the team in advancing performance. After watching, the team informally discusses relevance. This is brilliant on many levels. Think about what this generates!

1. The assigned employee spends time researching topics they feel are important to the team's performance. Think of the learning that occurred as part of that process!
2. The leader gains tremendous insight as to what the team members are seeing as areas that need to be discussed.
3. The team members have meaningful discussion on a wide array of work-related topics that the leader may not have even had on the radar.
4. Ideas generated as a result of the discussion provide both inspiration and hope, for everyone involved.

Book Club

Assign a book or magazine article and plan a meeting (or series of meetings) to discuss. Tips:

- The entire meeting should be devoted to the assigned topic. If doing several meetings on the same book, keep meetings short. You might consider planning a retreat type meeting for short books or articles.

- Divide reading into reasonable segments for discussion.

- Make it fun! Be creative in how you incorporate lessons into everyday tasks. Consider an employee poster contest or other creative outlet.

- Choose material you believe to be important and relevant. Be sure it is applicable to all team members.

The Match Game

Brainstorm with your team to identify topics of interest and need. Then work behind the scenes to match an internal employee who is an expert (or perhaps, who needs an incentive to become an expert). Tips:

- Create a master list of topics from the brainstorm session that you will include based on your thoughts, opinions, and available internal expertise.

- Target topics that can be done effectively with 15 to 30 minutes of content. When scheduling the meeting series, allow time for discussion and questions.

- Work to include everyone. This is a lesson for you in delegation – in other words, don't always choose the person you consider to be most competent and trustworthy.

- Announce topics and dates in advance and require all employees to be ready for the discussion. Consider giving them a reading assignment prior to the meeting (ask the assigned "expert" for their recommendations).

- Share widely the topics that are included in this project and the experts who will lead the charge. Consider a huge poster that is visible to all. This will remind your employees that these topics were *their* ideas, and that you are working to meet their needs.

Brown Bag Lunch with the Boss

Invite employees to attend lunch with the boss, once monthly. Tips:

- You can either fulfill this as THE boss, or consider asking your boss to be THE boss.

- Make sure folks understand this is informal. Bring your own brown bag lunch and invite them to do the same.

- Don't create a formal agenda. This is a time for you to listen. To prepare, take time to think through current happenings and be ready to answer hard questions.

- Use this as an opportunity to help employees understand how their specific work is advancing the organization's ability to fulfill the mission and vision.

- Consider looking for openings to praise employees for good work. Negative feedback is not to be done in this format.

Personal Random Development Challenge (PRDC)

Ask each person on your team to choose one area in which they need to improve their skills and achieve personal growth. Then challenge them to do something about it in a very short time frame – without spending money. Tips:

- Schedule a PRDC Presentation Showcase. Make a big deal out of this session by announcing the date at the time of announcing the project. Schedule ample time for everyone to make a brief presentation.

- Explain that each person will be asked to "teach back." They will be asked to present what they learn to the rest of the team.

- Keep presentation requirements simple. Allow employees to present in ways that meet their comfort level – including formats such as group discussion, assessments, games, presentations, and lecture.

- Keep presentation times short – perhaps ten minutes to present followed by ten minutes of group discussion. You decide – just be sure to announce this as part of the requirements for presenting.

- Allow each person to choose their topic. Do not assign topics. Remember, this is about personal development – which means the topic needs to be personal to the employee.

- Consider recording the Showcase and sharing short segments on organizational learning sites.

Targeted Assignment

When an employee has been given the opportunity to attend a formal training opportunity, reap the benefits by giving them a targeted assignment. The assignment is to come back and share key insights related to the training objectives. Tips:

- This can easily be done as part of a staff meeting and in a very short time frame.

- Ensure the employee goes to the training knowing he or she will be expected to share skills learned.

- Consider giving them a written assignment before they attend training, such as:

  I hope you enjoy your training session next week on Improving Workplace Relationships. It sounds interesting! While there, please keep track of what you find to be the five most important points. I will ask you to share them at our next staff meeting. Have fun!

Conclusion

For the leader, one thing is clear when it comes to talent development: you must model continuous learning. Be the expert your title says you are!

Stay on top of your game. Read the latest books and know the latest trends. Consider how this information impacts your workplace and your industry.

Then to model your efforts toward continuous learning:

- Share relevant content with employees. If you come across something that is of interest to any one person on your staff, share it.

- When it is time for celebration, give books or other learning opportunities as gifts.

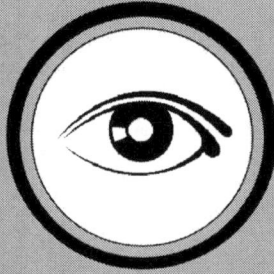

9. DEVELOPING A SUPERVISORY MINDSET

"With great power comes great responsibility."

Uncle Ben - Spiderman

There are many challenges facing a first-time supervisor. Roles change, as do relationships. The new supervisor will need to look at things in new and unexpected ways There is a big change in perspective.

The first-time supervisor may not be adequately prepared for the new role. Training needed for new duties may not be readily available. The new supervisor needs support and the support system may be lacking, or nonexistent.

First-time supervisors accept their new position with enthusiasm and optimism. Often, people who become supervisors were promoted because they were outstanding employees who delivered great results.

Suddenly, delivering great results depends on something completely different – *the ability to get results through others.*

There are three essential skills that will help new supervisors survive the first months of transition. These three essential skills provide an area of focus in a wide field of important supervisory skills. They give the first-time supervisor a solid place to start.

1. **Supervisors must learn how to flip their perspective.** This includes expanding personal knowledge and understanding of the organization to form a management point of view. To get results through others, supervisors need to understand how to set goals and expectations, establish priorities, use personal power, and include employees in problem solving and decision making.

2. **Supervisors need to employ effective communication and listening skills.** This includes both oral and written communication techniques. Methods of communicating must also be considered including holding effective staff meetings, completing one-on-ones with employees, and specifics on communicating with internal and external customers.

3. **Supervisors must build effective relationships and use those relationships for help and support.** A supervisor needs to have strong relationships with his or her

employees and also with peers, bosses, and customers. Learning how to foster those relationships is critical. The ability to manage a high performing work team depends on knowing how to build effective relationships.

Without question, new supervisors need training in many skill areas, but they need more than just training. New supervisors need support, mentoring, and time to develop skills and knowledge.

MUST DO'S IN MAKING THE TRANSITION

- Recognize and accept the fact that your role has changed.
- Strike a balance between over control and under control.
- Develop a support team, including your manager, your peers, and your family.
- Begin to **think** like a supervisor.
- Flip your perspective. ME now becomes WE! Some examples:
  - ➢ Leaders are long-term thinkers. This means you must expand your thinking to include the future of your organization.
  - ➢ Leaders have interests in their own organization beyond those of their own work units.
  - ➢ Leaders have strong political skills. You can no longer hide from organizational politics.

➤ Leaders do not accept the status quo. They constantly seek innovative solutions for improvement.

➤ Leaders heavily emphasize vision, values, and motivation.

Many of the skills needed to develop the supervisory mindset are included in guides throughout this book! If you are trying to figure out where to start, begin with these!

- Communication

- Delegation

- Empowering Employees

- Meeting with Staff

- Setting Expectations

ME BECOMES WE.

10. EMAIL WRITING

FOR SUCCESS

Email is one of our primary communication methods. We spend hours writing and reading Email. Mastering the art of writing Email can save time and frustration for both the writer and its reader.

Email Rules to Live By:

1. Write the Email for the intended AUDIENCE – understanding that the audience you intend may not be the audience that receives your message. Don't forget that Email messages are easily (and sometimes thoughtlessly) forwarded. Writing a message to an external customer is very different from writing a message to your coworker.

When addressing your message, decide where to address each recipient.

TO:	This is your primary target. Write your message to that person or persons. Think about how much they know – or don't know. Tailor you message to their preferences when you can.
CC:	This is your secondary target. CC stands for "Courtesy Copy." It does not invite the addressee(s) to respond – so don't expect a response.
BCC:	This should seldom be used – if ever. It is often used in writing a message to a list of people whose Email addresses must remain confidential.

2. Start your message with the PURPOSE. Ask yourself this question: "Why am I writing this?" The answer to that question is the first line of your Email. Tell your reader first thing, what this is about. Remember, if you don't hook them in the first line or two, they likely will not read the message all the way through.

3. Be SPECIFIC. We often wonder why our Email doesn't give us the response we need – the answer is that quite often, we don't ask for the response we need. For example, telling me you need something done ASAP means different things to different people. If you need it Monday at noon, say "I need this Monday at noon."

4. Use BULLETED LISTS.

   a. Bulleted lists convey information in an easy-to-read format.

b. They help the writer organize information into logical order and to shorten messages and get to the point.

c. Seeing information as bullets helps the reader more accurately and quickly understand.

d. If a response is needed, it is much easier for the reader to respond to specific points.

5. Always use a friendly professional TONE. Humor sounds like sarcasm. Anger and threats do not belong in the Email world. To ensure a neutral friendly tone every time, use the three steps for organizing Email described below.

The way you open and close your message is important. Begin with a short greeting: "Hello Bob." The close should be brief: "Thank you." A neutral greeting and close adds to friendly tone.

Emoji's, cute backgrounds, and colorful fonts do not belong in business Email. Their use does not convey an appropriate tone for business. ☹

6. Keep it SHORT – but not so short that the tone is unfriendly. If you need to write a long Email, consider making it a Word document and attaching it to the Email. We now know that our brain needs white space so, use reasonable sized fonts, keep paragraphs short, and don't be afraid to use tables and other formatting tools to help your reader quickly find what they need.

7. Organizing Email messages into THREE PARTS will solve most problems with tone, giving too much or too little information, and giving specific instructions. This is presented as Open, Middle, Close.

OPEN	Purpose – here's what this message is about. Can be done in one to two sentences.	Hi Jon. Here are the promised instructions on how to write friendly, professional Email messages.
MIDDLE	Use a bulleted list to give specific information you need to convey.	1. Start with the purpose – tell them what this is about or answer their question, first thing. 2. Use a bulleted list to give them specific information. 3. Close with instructions on what to do next. Be specific.
CLOSE	Tell them specifically what you need and by when. Give your contact information if needed.	Thanks for your interest Jon and please know that no response is needed to this message. If you have questions, call me direct at 555-555-5555.

Be aware, that many messages can be conveyed in one short paragraph. Just be sure the paragraph opens with purpose, puts needed details in the middle, and ends with specific instructions.

11. EMPOWERING EMPLOYEES

To empower means to give official authority, to enable, to promote the self-actualization of others.

To empower others, you will need to give them tools to help them to be problem solvers and feel they are in control. Here's how:

1. **TEACH**

   Teach your employees to be problem solvers. Insist they come to you with suggestions to solve problems, instead of complaints. Give them a map to follow in solving problems – a template. You can use these classic steps (below) in problem solving, or modify the steps to meet your needs.

CLASSIC PROBLEM-SOLVING STEPS

1. Identify a problem.
2. Define and analyze.
3. Work at finding the root cause.
4. Explore solutions.
5. Implement the solution.
6. Evaluate the effectiveness of the solution.

Teach employees to describe problems with specific facts. Remind them that simple solutions are often best. Help them to understand their role in solving problems.

2. ASK QUESTIONS

Help employees solve problems on their own by asking the right questions. Try using these prompts in guiding your discussion:

A. Describe the problem. Be specific and tell me the facts.

B. What is the simplest solution you can think of to solve this problem?

C. How will this solution take care of the problem? How will it help us?

D. What steps are you willing to take to put this solution into motion?

E. What help, support, or involvement would you like to receive from me?

3. HELP EMPLOYEES FEEL IN CONTROL

- Give employees multiple and structured ways to communicate.

- Be honest with what you know, don't know, and can't say.

- Make meetings feel safe.

- Act on feedback.

- When possible, create employee teams to solve problems.

- When you delegate, do it right! (Refer to "Delegation" guide number 7.)

- Always follow up.

"Empowerment is about letting go
so that others can get going."

-Ken Blanchard

12. FEEDBACK

Feedback can be both positive and negative. Generally, it is easier to give positive feedback than negative. Surprisingly, neither is routinely delivered in most workplaces.

As a boss, you will need to let people know when they are doing good work. People need to feel valued. (Refer to "Appreciation," guide number 1.) Positive feedback must be a conscious effort and at the same time, be genuine.

You will also need to address problems. That is uncomfortable. We would prefer to keep things peaceful. Yet, when problems are not addressed there are dire results: poor performance goes unchecked; valuable resources are wasted; top performers become disengaged; and expectations are unclear – and unmet. Managers must be able to give constructive feedback.

Constructive Feedback when There is a Problem

Offering constructive feedback doesn't have to be hard. In fact, a manager who builds in timely feedback may succeed in building a culture where feedback is accepted and welcomed – even desired.

It's true that people in general, want to do good work – and they want specifics on how to deliver better results. One important point, when you deliver constructive feedback, focus on problems – don't make it personal.

STEPS

1. Set it up – "I'd like to discuss . . . "

2. Describe what was *observed.* Remember to:

   a. Stick with facts.

   b. Be specific.

   c. Focus on problems.

   d. Use positive words.

3. Explain why this is not okay. In other words, explain why the problem is a problem.

4. Ask for their thoughts.

5. Ask – then confirm or explain – how they can change their behavior to correct the problem (be specific).

6. Summarize and give support.

Five Powerful Words

1. **Option:**
   "Let's explore some options . . ."

2. **Idea:**
   "What ideas do you have for solving this?"

3. **Recommendation:**
   "What is your recommendation?"

4. **Suggestion:**
   "I am open for your suggestions."

5. **Solution:**
   "What solution do you propose?"

THINGS TO CONSIDER

- Invite regular dialogue about what's working – and not working – and then listen. It is important to hear your employee's perspectives on what is and isn't working. You may be surprised.

- When analyzing how you will deliver feedback, first consider how systems and processes are impacting the problem, before blaming it on people.

- Keep your "finger on the pulse" – know what's happening in your workplace. Consider eating lunch in a common area or doing some work in the middle of the action. Pay attention to what is going on around you.

- Acknowledge mistakes – especially your own.

- Holding people accountable is a responsibility of a leader.

13. LEADER OR MANAGER?

Leaders and managers are suffering from an identity crisis — are they leaders or managers? Is there a difference? In fact, there is. Consider these definitions.

Leadership: The ability to influence, motivate, and direct others to obtain desired objectives.

Management: Planning, organizing, leading, and controlling the people working in an organization and the ongoing set of tasks and activities they perform.

Leaders and managers do have different skills sets. By definition we can conclude that leadership focuses on people and managers focus on tasks. It's not that simple.

In reality we know that the two definitions cross. Seldom do we find a person who is a pure leader – or a pure manager in the true sense of the definition. This is a good thing as leaders who cannot manage – and managers who cannot lead, can be disastrous. An organization needs both great leadership and great management to succeed.

Best bosses understand the difference between leadership and management and can employ both skills sets as needed.

Think about it. Leaders are known for having great vision (big picture thinking), an ability to see the future of their organization. If they do not understand the management side of things, they very well may lose sight of what needs to be done to execute. Managers are known to organize work, to get things done in an organization, and to ensure compliance. If managers can only focus on what needs to be done right now, they may lose sight of purpose.

Look around and you will likely see examples of great leaders who have tremendous vision but cannot figure out how to turn the lights on in the building. We also see examples of great managers who get stuck in "management land" and become complacent and sometimes outright depressed.

Leaders and managers who are able to employ both skill sets become great bosses and are known to:

- Manage the operations of the organization at a higher level of success.
- Make better decisions.

- See the "big picture" more clearly.

- Sustain higher performance over time.

- Welcome and use feedback from all sources.

- Get results!

LEADER – MANAGER COMPETENCIES

The following chart presents competencies for leaders and for managers. This will help you see the differences between the two.

As you read the chart, consider doing a self-assessment. Put a checkmark in one column or the other to indicate which of the two behaviors you most often display. This will give you a sense of whether you are leaning too heavily on either leadership or management.

LEADER	MANAGER
Has a long-range perspective.	Has a short-range perspective.
Asks *what* and *why.*	Plans *how* and *when.*
Eyes the horizon.	Eyes the bottom line.
Originates.	Imitates others.
Challenges the status quo.	Accepts the status quo.
Does the correct thing.	Does things correctly.
Seeks change.	Seeks continuity (stability).
Focuses on goals of innovation.	Focuses on goals for improvement.
Power is based on personal influence.	Power is based on position or authority.
Demonstrates skill in selling the vision.	Demonstrates skill in technical competence.
Demonstrates skill in dealing with ambiguity.	Demonstrates skill in administration.
Demonstrates skill in persuasion.	Demonstrates skill in supervision.
Works toward employee commitment.	Works toward employee compliance.
Plans strategy.	Plans tactics.
Sets policy.	Sets standard operating procedures.

Relies on intuitive decision-making style.	Relies on analytical decision-making style.
Takes the necessary risks.	Is risk cautious.
Uses a "transformational" communication style.	Uses a "transactional" communication style.
Uses an informational base, including "gut" feelings.	Mostly uses an informational base of data and facts.
Builds success through employee commitment.	Builds success through maintenance of quality.
Does not want to experience inertia (apathy).	Does not want to experience anarchy (chaos).
Develops the vision and the strategies to achieve it.	Plans, budgets, and designs detail steps.
Sets standards of excellence.	Sets standards of performance.
Develops the future direction by gathering future trends.	Develops the detailed plan to achieve results.

If you struggled with putting a check mark in one column or the other, you may be practicing as a best boss! Best bosses will be able to say that the answer depends on the situation!

14. MEETINGS WITH STAFF

A CHECKLIST

Meetings are often considered one of the primary sources of wasted time! Too bad, because when done right, they are one of the most effective tools a boss has in running an effective operation. It is essential that you are meeting regularly as a team and that when you meet, you are productive.

Defining the purpose of the meeting and preparing an actionable agenda are two critical components of running a productive meeting that are often overlooked by bosses.

PURPOSE

First, decide what specific purpose your meeting will have. If the purpose is simply to share information or communicate news, why have a meeting? Send an Email!

For example:

- AGENDA ITEM: New Policy

  Meet to discuss how to specifically implement a new policy. Don't meet to review what an employee can read on paper or online. Require that the policy be reviewed before the meeting. Then discuss only the sections that need clarification. The purpose of the meeting is not "New Policy." The purpose of the meeting is to define how to implement the new policy.

- AGENDA ITEM: Customer Service

  Meet to discuss ways to improve customer service. Don't meet to review a report that shows statistics indicating you need to improve customer service. The purpose of the meeting is to develop action steps to improve customer service.

- AGENDA ITEM: Budget Cuts

  Meet to discuss how to absorb the cuts without cutting services or people. Do not meet to cry in your bucket over something you can't control. The purpose of the meeting is to develop an action plan for absorbing new budget cuts.

AGENDA

An agenda is your written plan for the meeting. Your agenda:

- ➤ States the purpose of the meeting.
- ➤ Guides the meeting toward accomplishing the purpose by keeping the discussion on task.
- ➤ Ensures you meet defined and desired outcomes.

Use this checklist to ensure you are leading effective meetings.

BEFORE

- ☐ Define specific purpose. What will be your expectation for the successful conclusion of the meeting?
- ☐ Write agenda. Include purpose on agenda.
- ☐ Invite only those who have a role in accomplishing the meeting purpose. Don't require people to sit through a meeting if the purpose does not apply to them.

DURING

- ☐ Set ground rules with the group. As part of this define:
  - Who is participating and why.
  - Start and stop times (specific).
  - The meeting process – in other words, how will you reach decisions and identify action steps?
- ☐ Define roles
  - Appoint facilitator to keep conversation flowing equally and to watch meeting time. (Note: meeting must begin and end on time.)
  - Consider appointing someone to keep a list of action items as you move through discussions. Specifically, what will be done after the meeting, by whom, and when?
- ☐ Involve all participants and make them feel valued. Call on those who are quiet and probe when a message is unclear.
- ☐ Before ending, review action list and confirm understanding of what will happen next.

AFTER

☐ Do follow-up communication as needed with those who were there (and with those who were not.)

☐ Follow-up on the action list. Ensure tasks are completed as agreed during the meeting and that appropriate progress is being made in the meantime.

☐ Send a copy of the action list to all participants and interested parties, within two business days (sooner is better).

SAMPLE AGENDA

1. Welcome and Introductions*
2. Meeting Purpose
3. Item 1
4. Item 2
5. Summary
6. Action Item Review

*[NOTE: DON'T SKIP THIS. PEOPLE NEED A MINUTE TO GET FOCUSED – TO SHIFT THEIR MINDS TO THE TASK AT HAND.]

EXAMPLE
1. Welcome and Introductions
2. Purpose: Review the new budget and produce implementable ideas for saving money without cutting people.
3. The New Budget
4. Ideas for Saving Money
    1. Brainstorm
    2. Evaluate Ideas
5. Summary
6. What's Next

15. MEETING WITH EMPLOYEES ONE-ON-ONE

I often have leaders tell me that they don't have time to have regular meetings with their staff. In return, I offer that the most important part of their job is to take care of their staff! How can they ensure they are getting top performance if they are not taking time to know the people that work with them, and to understand their struggles, their goals, their current needs?

After all, what is the job of a leader? **The job of a leader is to get the work done through others.** They must find ways to communicate expectations, trust, delegate, educate, and let go.

One-on-one meetings are the best tool a leader can use to improve overall performance of the organization. They actually become time savers, as you and your employee learn to hold non-urgent conversations for the meeting instead of constantly interrupting one another. These meetings, when done well, serve to motivate, engage, and inspire your employees.

WHAT IS A ONE-ON-ONE?

This is simply an appointment – one-on-one – with an employee. This time is dedicated to that employee. It must be at a set time, on a set schedule. When you take time to meet with just one employee, it says to that person that they are important, that you care, and that you value them.

To succeed, you must emphasize the value and importance by keeping the appointment and establishing guidelines for the time together. Here's how it works.

1. **Two Agendas!** The number one agenda is set by the employee – and they go first. Start with their agenda which will include what they need to talk about. The number two agenda is yours. Have your agenda ready to cover the status of their work and special projects. (This is an excellent way for you to consistently give feedback on performance.)

   Issue this challenge to the employee: "See if you can cover everything I have on my agenda, before it's my turn." In other words, allow your employee the opportunity to cover the topics they find to be most important. This will tell you a lot!

2. **Scheduling** is sometimes a challenge. How often should you do one-on-ones? How long should they last?

   Frequency is dependent on several factors such as: How many employees do you have? Are your employees onsite? Obviously, the number of people you supervise will impact the number of one-on-ones you can schedule in any one-time period.

   Experience levels are also key in determining frequency. New employees would ideally have a meeting with you every week – maybe even every day for the first week or two. Employees with more experience also need one-on-ones but not as frequently – once each month should be enough unless they have a new assignment or specific need.

3. **Meeting Specifics:**
   a. It is important to set a start and stop time and stick to it no matter what! If you find that the meeting time established is too short or too long, adjust the time for future one-on-ones.
   b. Do not allow interruptions and do not cancel on the employee.
   c. Meet in a private area. Consider meeting over coffee or in an area that is outside the immediate work area.
   d. The meeting duration will vary with the employee's experience level. If you are working with a new employee and meeting with them daily, five to fifteen minutes is enough. An experienced employee who meets with you once monthly, may need thirty to sixty minutes.

BEST PRACTICES

1. Set up a one-on-one folder for each employee. Include:

   a. Latest performance appraisal including any goals and objectives in play.

   b. Any information relevant to this employee – performance notes, compliments, problems, articles to discuss, etc.

2. Stop yourself from running to the employee with any issue that comes to your desk. If it is not urgent – and often it really isn't – put it in the employee's one-on-one folder and discuss it as part of your next meeting.

3. Set up a regular meeting time with each person, if possible. Stick to it! Don't cancel unless absolutely unavoidable.

4. When you meet, always allow the employee to go first. Expect them to come with an agenda.

5. Review the contents of your one-on-one folder since your last meeting – this most likely serves as your agenda.

6. Teach your employees to create a reciprocal one-on-one folder for you. The contents (including their notes) most likely serve as their agenda!

7. Discuss projects, performance, goals, etc.

8. Discuss specific ideas for improving performance.

9. Use this as an opportunity to praise and redirect.

10. Keep notes – this will serve you well when it is appraisal time!

16. MOMENTUM

CREATING AND MAINTAINING

Momentum

Strength or force gained by motion or by a series of events.

Momentum is about pace. How many times have you seen a big launch party – ideas with great promise – just fizzle out. Or, a special project is introduced and we start off excited and motivated. There's a sense of urgency and we devise a plan to meet every two weeks to keep our project moving forward.

Then, something happens and we cancel a meeting. Over time, we lose momentum and when we lose momentum, we lose the excitement, motivation, and passion to keep moving forward.

There is much to be said for creating and maintaining high momentum. A sense of urgency helps us to achieve timely goals and outcomes. A desire to get things done quickly – to be successful, works in our favor.

The role of a boss is to push, just enough, to keep people excited about an initiative. When we keep momentum high, both productivity and employee engagement improve. People see results and feel a sense of achievement.

Tips for Creating Momentum

- Keep the pace high. Meet with employees often – possibly daily!

- Create and feed a sense of urgency.

- Insist cancelled meetings be rescheduled and promptly held.

- Help employees prioritize their work so they can stay on top of projects.

- Use your Team Cheer to keep people focused. (Refer to "Vision" guide number 25.)

- Set the example for your employees – they look to you for clues on how to behave.

- Have frequent team conversations about the progress you are observing.

- Reward behavior that you see that you'd like to see again.

17. MOTIVATION

Motivation: Forces acting either on or within a person to initiate behavior. All behavior is motivated by needs. Can it be this simple?

Needs → Behavior → Satisfaction

The truth is that you can't really motivate anyone other than yourself. Motivation, true motivation, comes from within. Many theorists argue that motivation is based on satisfaction of needs – how can you possibly know the needs of every employee? Sometimes, we are not even sure of our own needs!

HOW TO IDENTIFY EACH EMPLOYEE'S NEEDS

Pay attention, pay attention, pay attention. Then ask. Know that you cannot always apply group solutions – each individual is different.

WHAT CAN YOU DO?

- Identify needs and use that knowledge to create an environment in which employees can self-motivate.

- Help employees to understand their personal strengths and passions and give them opportunities to use them.

- Show genuine appreciation for good work. (Refer to "Appreciation" guide number 1.)

- Define and communicate expectations.

- Manage resources – check that employees have what they need to do their work effectively.

- Include employees in decision making – help them be part of the solution instead of part of the problem. Ask for their opinion.

- Address problems in the workplace. Failure to address problems (especially performance issues) is a huge demotivator for employees.

- Show that you care and encourage them from your heart.

18. PERFORMANCE APPRAISAL

A PROCESS

Many managers admit that writing performance appraisals is dreadful. Why is this a difficult task? Well, you are being asked to judge another person. Not only will you write down what you think of the person's performance, you'll have to justify your thoughts and show this document to that person!

Here's how it often works. You realize it is time for the performance appraisal. You scramble to put together information to cover the period of time included in the appraisal. It is not easy to pull together information for a whole block of time. Too often, the appraisal is written purely from memory and the form is filled out merely to complete a requirement.

Here's a simple process that will make doing performance appraisal easy. The result: no more disagreements with employees about their performance, a factual evaluation, and no surprises.

THREE PHASES OF THE PERFORMANCE APPRAISAL CYCLE

PHASE 1 **PLANNING** Period at beginning of process – for new employee about 1 month – for others, even shorter.	TO DO: 1. *Organize*, prepare, and update required forms (don't forget the job description). 2. *Define* methods for collecting data, meeting with the employee, and expectations for employee reporting. 3. *Meet* with employee and review the job description, evaluation form. Agree on objectives and expectations.
PHASE 2 **MANAGEMENT** This is the longest period in the process because it includes all the time in between planning and actual evaluation.	TO DO: 1. *Collect data.* Create a one-on-one folder for each employee and include newly created goals, relevant memos, reports, and information. (See more on one-on-one folders in "Meeting with Employees One-on-one" in guide number 14.)

	2. *Document* throughout. Keep notes in your folders regarding performance. Entries can be just one line and should be statements of fact.
	3. *Meet regularly* with the employee. Set up one-on-one meetings and keep discussions going throughout this phase of the process.
PHASE 3 EVALUATION	TO DO: 1. *Compile data.* Review your notes and inserts in the one-on-one file. 2. *Invite* your employee to give input. 3. *Prepare* a positive/negative list to help you in being specific about performance. 4. *Write* the evaluation. For narrative, use plain language and use facts, not opinion. 5. *Meet* with the employee uninterrupted. Discuss performance and begin discussion of objectives for the next cycle. 6. Have employee *sign* then forward as needed. 7. Go back to Phase 1!

EIGHT TOP TIPS

1. Appraisals are important, treat them with importance.

2. Prepare at the start of the cycle. Organize, define methods and expectations, and communicate with your employee.

3. Manage the process throughout by collecting data, documenting, and communicating.

4. At evaluation time, write in plain language, set specific goals, and include your employee.

5. Perform periodic checks to make sure objectives are still applicable.

6. Use specific statements and examples to back up your ratings.

7. Involve your employees throughout the process.

8. Never underestimate the value of this process, and your role.

Many of the skills needed for completing the Performance Appraisal process are included in guides throughout this book. If you are trying to figure out where to start, begin with these!

- Coaching, Counseling, and Mentoring
- Communication
- Feedback
- Meeting with Employees One-on-One
- Setting Expectations

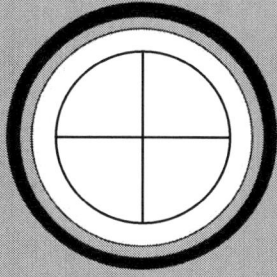

19. PERSONALITIES

UNDERSTANDING AND FLEXING

As a boss, you will work with a variety of people – and personalities. Interestingly, extensive research has shown that there are distinct personality styles that humans share – and it is not impossible to understand natural personality traits. By learning about the priorities, motivations, fears, limitations, and strengths of the people around you, you will come to understand how to flex your style and build more effective relationships.

In 1928, Dr. William Marston published his book "Emotions of Normal People." He introduced us to four primary emotions and identified behaviors associated with those emotions. Marston's work is known to many as DISC – Dominance, Influence, Steadiness, and Conscientiousness.

Today, there are many assessments available to help us understand personalities. Whether you use Marston's model or any of the many personality assessments available, it is important to first identify and understand your own natural behaviors and strengths. Then, you can begin to understand the natural behaviors and strengths of the people around you – which means **we can predict behavior**. This is fascinating and exciting!

When we know the natural strengths and challenges our employees possess, we are equipped to use their strengths to produce engaged, motivated, happy employees. Most people will naturally seek work where they feel most comfortable – the place where they can do what they are good at doing.

MARSTON'S THEORY

Using Marston's theory, we know what general traits exist for the four styles he defined:

DOMINANCE	INFLUENCE
Quick to act	Quick to act
Fast paced	Accepting and trusting
Questioning	Social
Direct	Talkative
Results oriented	Team oriented
CONSCIENTIOUSNESS	**STEADINESS**
Slower to act	More moderate pace
Skeptical	Accepting and trusting
Analytical	Good listener
Like to work alone	Indecisive
Process oriented	Relationship oriented

Think about the people on your team and you can most likely, use this chart alone to predict what their natural style might be. Of course, it is better to complete a full DISC assessment than to rely on this chart alone!

WHAT WE KNOW

- We need all styles in an organization. Why? Because we need all of the different strengths these different styles offer.
- No one style is good or bad. We know that styles alone do not "make" a person or "break" them.
- Style alone does not predict failure or success. If a person does not have a natural strength that is needed for a position, it doesn't mean they cannot do it.
- Everyone has a little of all styles within them.
- People can "flex." Flexing happens when a person purposely adjusts his or her style so that he or she can better communicate with someone of another style.

FLEXING YOUR STYLE

Once we understand styles – and the styles of those around us, we can successfully adjust our style to improve relationships and achieve better outcomes.

As an example, think of that person who just loves details and tends to question everything. Of course, someone else has a style that is the exact opposite. The opposite styled person does not like details. Instead, they see big picture ideas and don't want to get dragged into the muck. Quite simply, this person sees the beautiful forest as one big picture – the other person sees each beautiful tree, in detail.

To flex styles, the big picture person will need to be prepared to communicate with the detail-oriented person, and visa-versa. The big picture person will need to express their ideas with precision and perhaps show documentation that supports facts. The detail-oriented person will need to allow the big picture person to verbalize their ideas and hold back from the need to ask so many questions in succession.

When we flex, benefits begin to surface:

- The quality of interactions will improve.

- People will relax and be more receptive.

- Tensions will ease and conflict will be reduced.

- There is a better chance for open discussion.

- It's all about improving your work life – and just may make the world a better place!

AS A BOSS

Workplace relationships are often a factor in the success or failure of important outcomes. As a boss, you can take this knowledge of personality differences and expand your knowledge – and that of your employees – to make your workplace a happier and more productive place to be. Remember, we need the natural strengths of all types of people, which means we need to understand styles and teach people how to flex personal behaviors.

20. PRESENTATIONS

While public speaking is scary for the majority of the population, making presentations is part of life in any leadership role.

Many leaders make presentations almost daily and some don't realize that is what they are doing! A presentation can be a formal talk to a group where you present information. You may have handouts or other supporting material. Sometimes presentations can be more informal – almost like a group discussion or facilitation.

Either way, when you are the one delivering information, selling a new process, explaining how things work, giving instructions, or talking in front of any number of people, you are in essence, making a presentation.

Here are three steps to simplify the process of making a presentation, along with some suggestions for doing it well.

STEP 1 – DEVELOP YOUR CONTENT

Develop your content means to prepare in advance. Who will be in your audience? What needs to be included? To help you in choosing content:

1. *Identify your audience.* Think about the people who will be listening to you. At what level is their knowledge and interest? Your presentation will need to appeal to people who have varied levels of both.

2. *Clarify your purpose.* Be sure your purpose is clear – and that the clarity is conveyed to your audience. As you work on what to include, throw out any content that does not align with your purpose.

3. *Start with what you know,* then research.

4. *Decide on main points.* (For example: "Three Critical Issues," "Five Reasons this Change Will Improve our Workplace.")

5. *Draft your outline* using these headings:

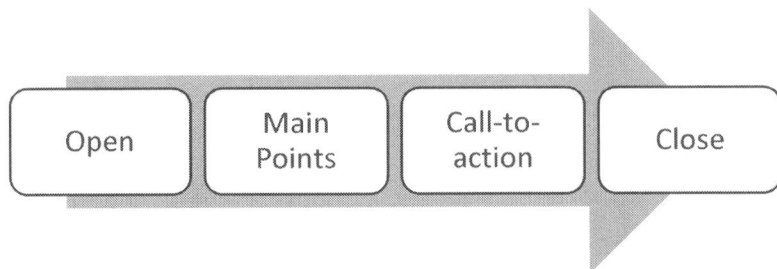

STEP 2 – DESIGN YOUR PRESENTATION

Next is to organize the information you will include. There are several pieces to consider such as the speech itself, your notes, handouts, activities, and visual aids.

ORGANIZING CONTENT

- Once you have identified and outlined main points and sub-points, work on structure.
- Structure must be clear and logical (Time order? Topic order? Problem-solution?)
- Plan for transitions between points. They must be smooth and effective so the presentation flows.
- Plan your opening and closing (for tips see Step 3 below).

USING POWERPOINT

We have all heard the phrase "Death by PowerPoint." PowerPoint presentations can be terrible – but when done correctly they are highly effective.

Keys to success:

- Limit the information on each slide. Try not to include more than three bullet points in one slide.
- Consider using a picture show. Remember that many people are visual learners. The picture will help them connect to your point and latch on. The picture used must be relevant to the topic.
- Remember the slides are for your audience, not you. Do not use the slides to read from during the presentation. Reading a slide verbatim is never okay.

- Use care with colors and backgrounds, keep it simple and easy to see.
- Use fonts that are at least 32 point.
- Never use the PowerPoint slide handout as a handout for your presentation. Two reasons:
  1. If the slides have enough information within to tell the story of your presentation in words, then why bother to make the presentation? Just give them the handout.
  2. If there is text, a picture, or a chart on the slide, it will likely be too small to read in the handout format.

FACILITATING ACTIVITIES

Activities such as games, discussion groups, assessments, demonstrations, simulations, and other exercises can be fun and effective! They can also be a disaster.

The type of presentation you are making is key to deciding whether any of these activities are relevant. If you are training, you will need to include activities to keep your audience engaged and to draw from their experience as adult learners. If you are presenting a proposal to your management team, activities may not be appropriate.

If you plan to make a presentation in which you use activities of any type, do your research. Think through potential problems. Consider whether every audience member will be able to participate without limitations. There are also materials and equipment issues to work out. It's best to rehearse if possible, try it out first.

STEP 3 – DELIVER YOUR MESSAGE

- Take care of details before your presentation begins, such as:

  - ➤ Room set-up.
  - ➤ Equipment set-up. Test the projector, remote, computer, visuals, sound, video, and screen.

- Start with an *opening* that will get your audience's attention right away! Ideas for great openings include:

  - ➤ Using powerful quotes or statistics.
  - ➤ What-if scenarios.
  - ➤ Analogies.
  - ➤ Telling a relevant story.

- Make your *purpose* known from the start.

- *Involve others* when you can – remember to focus on what they are hearing, not what you are saying.

- *Facilitate!*

- *Listen* while you speak.

- Don't close with questions and answers (Q&A). Instead:

  - ➤ Stop **before** the closing and ask, "Before I close, what questions do you have?" Don't ask if there are any questions. Hear the difference?

  - ➤ Repeat all questions before you answer.

  - ➤ If the answer is lengthy, ask the questioner to see you after the session so that you can have a more in-depth conversation.

- In your *closing,* restate your main points. Ideas for great closings include:

> ➢ *A new surprising fact*

> ➢ *A provocative question*

> ➢ *A quote*

> ➢ *A return to your opening*

> ➢ *A final story*

MOST IMPORTANT – Many people are nervous to stand in front of the room and have everyone looking at them while they try to speak intelligently. Remember, it is not about you! If you are worried about the attention being on you then you have forgotten the most important truth of public speaking.

IT'S ALL ABOUT THE AUDIENCE, not you, not the visual aids, not even the words you speak. It's about what your audience is hearing, not what you are saying.

Performing Tips!

- Use the entire room.
- Watch your posture and non-verbals.
- Be natural – authentic – you.
- Make eye contact.
- Use silence. Allow time for people to think.
- Make sure they can hear you and see visuals.
- Move!

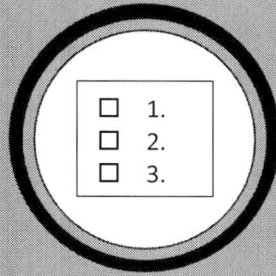

21. PRIORITIES

Because you have taken time to develop your vision and expectations, establishing priorities will be much easier for all. Great bosses do not assume that their employees understand priorities.

You will want to have regular conversations with each employee about their work tasks and how they should make decisions on how to prioritize.

During the conversation:

- Make it easy for them to talk with you about what is causing stress in their work.
- Ask them what new assignments they have taken on that you may not know about.

- Have them show you what projects are on their list of priorities. Help them adjust the list if needed.
- Help them determine how the tasks that are considered priorities, tie in to the big picture.

As the boss, keep your priority list up-to-date! Here are some tips for establishing priorities.

- Have a conversation with yourself, as described above!

- Set aside uninterrupted planning time.

- Work to identify and eliminate unnecessary work.

- Don't fall in to the "we've always done it this way" trap. There are often better ways to do things that we fail to consider.

- Find clever ways to include your staff in completing assignments.

If you are struggling with what is most important, try these questions:

What's most important – right now?

What task will have the most impact on business results?

What have you promised to do?

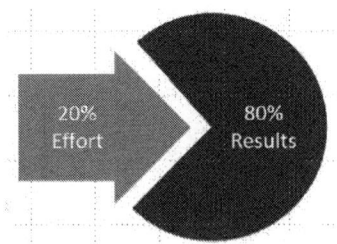

What tasks need to be done to meet deadlines?

20% Effort → 80% Results

Think about this: as much as 80% of your success today will come from 20% of the items on your to-do list.

22. SETTING EXPECTATIONS

A vocabulary lesson:

Goal: Broad statement of work to be accomplished in a given period of time.

Objective: Action item that helps achieve goals. Objectives help break down goals into workable chunks.

Expectation: A strong belief that someone will achieve a defined task.

> *"If you don't know where you are going,*
> *you'll end up someplace else."*
>
> *-Yogi Berra*

SETTING GOALS

We need goals – an understanding of what we are trying to accomplish. It is important to break your mission and vision down into something manageable. To guide you in writing goals that are clear, relevant, and achievable, use the well-known SMARTER goal criteria. Write your goal and then test it by asking, "Is this goal . . ."

S pecific

M easurable

A ctionable

R ealistic

T ime-bound

E thical

R ecorded

Ideas for Forming New Goals
▪ Words in Mission and Vision Statement
▪ Critical Job Responsibilities
▪ Position Descriptions
▪ Organizational and Department Goals

SETTING OBJECTIVES

Objectives are "mini" goals that help us achieve more long-term goals. Once we have a goal, we write objectives to break it down into manageable chunks. This serves to establish benchmarks, keep us focused on progress, and celebrate accomplishments more frequently!

Objectives can also use the SMARTER criteria to test their merit. Objectives are in fact goals.

Example: Goals and Objectives

PJ'S CONSTRUCTION COMPANY

Goal: Build and occupy a new company storage facility by the start of our next fiscal year.

Objectives:

1. Select final site location within one month.

2. Complete exterior structure within six months.

3. Complete interior structure within ten months.

4. Move all materials from corporate building into new space by end of month eleven.

SETTING EXPECTATIONS

You may be familiar with the Pygmalion Effect – a psychological phenomenon in which high expectations lead to improved performance. Some refer to this simply as a self-fulfilling prophecy. If we believe an employee can achieve great performance, they in fact do. If we believe an employee is incapable, they prove us right. Bottom line, as bosses we need to treat our employees in ways that lead to superior performance.

This puts pressure on you to set high expectations, believe in your people, and equip them with what they need to meet your high expectations.

Employees must clearly understand your expectations for their performance. You must communicate openly what you expect to be accomplished. Many times, bosses are unconsciously more effective in communicating low expectations than in communicating high expectations! You have most likely witnessed this.

SETTING PERFORMANCE EXPECTATIONS – TIPS

- Take time to make expectations clear in your mind, before you have a conversation with an employee.

- Remember that expectations start with a mindset, confidence that people can perform at a high level.

- Pay attention to the process of setting expectations, set your employee up for success from the start.

- Clearly communicate goals and objectives.

- Explain the "why." Help employees see the big picture.

- Personalize goals, objectives, and expectations with input from your employee. Get agreement, and commitment.

- Some areas will be hard to measure. Consider a range.

- Keep track and analyze available data.

- Communicate continuously.

- Modify later if necessary. It's okay to change a goal or objective if it is no longer the right thing.

- Reward, correct, or adjust as needed.

23. TEAMWORK

Team

Two or more people who come together for a common purpose and who are mutually accountable for results.

The number of resources available to give advice on working with teams indicate that this is a difficult subject. It is. Bringing together people with different personalities, different goals, different perspectives and asking them to focus on a single goal is inherently difficult.

Yet, the value of teams is immeasurable. Effective teams bring tremendous value to organizations. Effective teams are known to:

- Increase productivity.

- Do work that ordinary groups can't do.

- Make better use of resources.

- Improve communication.

- Find creative and effective solutions to problems.

- Make better decisions.

- Produce higher quality goods and services.

- Improve processes.

There are some amazing resources available to leaders today in helping work with team issues. For a deep dive into the subject, check out the work of Patrick Lencioni and Ken Blanchard. Lencioni has given us five behaviors that are essential for cohesive teams. Ken Blanchard has defined the seven characteristics of high performing teams.

To get started in understanding how to help your team work together effectively, there are three areas that deserve focus.

1. **PURPOSE** is clearly understood by all.

   Begin with mission – what are you trying to accomplish? What is the work of the team? How does the team's purpose fit into the overall mission of the organization? Every team must understand why they exist and how their results will contribute to the organization's success. Clarity must be a priority. Make no assumptions that people understand the purpose of the team and their role on the team.

For the team leader, this means providing clarity, opportunities for input and dialogue, and constantly reviewing the work of the team to ensure they are on track in working toward the purpose. It also means getting commitment from the members of the team.

2. **PEOPLE** must feel valued.

   Making people feel valued begins with the leader and is ultimately the responsibility of every individual on the team. We must be sure that people are empowered, trusted, accountable, and appreciated.

   We must also recognize that everyone is different. It is important to take some time to get to know each other – to understand the differences of people on the team. Time spent talking about how to work together to embrace differences, instead of being frustrated by them, is a worthwhile investment.

   For the team leader, this means providing individual feedback and encouragement; enthusiasm and optimism; flexibility and understanding. One thing that is vitally important is simple appreciation. It is alarming how many leaders forget to simply say thank you.

3. **RESULTS** are the focus.

   Effective teams solve problems, they reach conclusions, and they take action. They continuously complete tasks that take them progressively toward their goals. Success is celebrated in small steps throughout the life of the team and team accomplishments are celebrated!

For the team leader, this means providing structure, clear goals, constructive feedback, accountability, and persistent focus.

These principles apply to all teams. New team members come in excited and ready to jump in. To stay connected to the purpose, they need to be reminded periodically of what their purpose is – and why it is important. All people need to feel valued. They need to know that their time and talents are being used in important ways. Everyone needs to see results.

FIVE THINGS TO DO RIGHT AWAY to improve team performance:

1. Clearly communicate the purpose and priorities of the team (over and over).

2. Get support from each individual. Make sure everyone is going in the same direction.

3. Organize activities that help team members get to know (and trust) each other.

4. Teach employees to constructively hold each other accountable.

5. Schedule regular updates on progress, move toward results!

24. TIME MANAGEMENT

Time Management Defined

The ability to control how you spend the hours in your day to effectively accomplish your goals.

Time management rules that have worked for years no longer make sense. Time management is very personal. What works for one person may not work for another. The key is to be productive, and to focus on productivity. Here are some tips for shifting your focus from "time management" to "attention" management.

Attention management is the ability to keep focused on important and relevant tasks while avoiding distractions, in order to maximize productivity.

PROTECTING YOUR TIME

- Consider setting up appointments to block time to work on projects.

- Adopt the mindset – this appointment can't be moved!

- Learn how, and when to say "No."

- For requests from your boss, say yes then ask for clarification on other priorities.

- When your mind wanders, take a quick break and refocus.

- Build a bunker so you can stay put. In other words, make sure you have what you need to begin with instead of having to interrupt yourself continuously.

- Ask for support from your boss and coworkers when you are working on a project deadline.

MULTITASKING – The Truth

Humans cannot do multiple things simultaneously. We can shift our focus from one thing to the next with astonishing speed, but full focus is only on one thing at a time. In fact, even computers do not multitask, they have the ability to process at amazing speeds but only one piece of code at a time!

YOUR TECHNOLOGY – A PERSONAL CHECKLIST

Indicate below which things you might do to improve your use of technology.

- ☐ Take time to learn more about the use of the apps I use.

- ☐ Take time to learn more about the software I use.

- ☐ Stop downloading every app people recommend and first research the benefit and cost (time).

- ☐ Set up rules in Outlook, Gmail, and other servers.

- ☐ Use ring tones to help make quick audio decisions with my phone. (You can set up different ring tones for different people in your contacts.)

- ☐ Turn off notifications in Email, Facebook, and other applications.

- ☐ Learn to drag my Emails into calendar appointments (Outlook).

- ☐ Use Email to effectively communicate and acquire information. Work to improve your Email writing skills.

YOUR ENVIRONMENT

- ☐ Consider conducting an environmental analysis. What things in your environment are blocking your ability to be productive?

- ☐ Think about what is available to you that you may be overlooking!

- ☐ Find a way to discourage interruptions! Researchers estimate workers are interrupted every 11 minutes and then spend almost a third of their day recovering from those distractions.

CONSIDER YOUR PERSONAL TIMING AND ENERGY STYLES

Take time to consider – then use for your own benefit:

- When are you most productive?

- When is your energy highest? Lowest?

- When is the best time to work on Email vs. making phone calls?

- What time of day is best for meetings?

- What energizes you?

- Where is the best place for you to get work done?

YOUR WORKFLOW MANAGEMENT SYSTEM

- Create your own system, one that works for you.

- Make it something you can see, outside your own head!

- Keep it simple – uncluttered – intentional.

BE WILLING TO EXPERIMENT

The key is to try some different techniques. Some things may or may not work in a particular situation – that's okay! Try lots of different approaches – and really try them, don't declare it a failure after a few attempts. Give new approaches time to work. And, consider asking someone else to help you evaluate whether it is working!

"When people work often matters as much as what they do."

-Daniel Pink

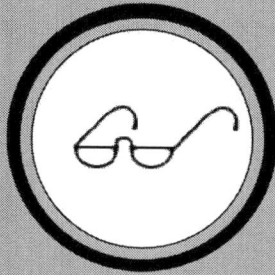

25. VISION

MAKING IT PERSONAL

Often, the mission and vision of the organization are already "on the wall." Many managers make the mistake of thinking that is enough – task complete – read it and move on. Not so fast.

Are YOU clear on the mission and mission of the organization? Start there! Remember that mission defines the purpose of the organization. Vision is more of an aspiration, where we hope to be in the future.

Vision is much bigger than the words on the wall. Every manager has their own vision – sometimes it is hard to put in to words – often because we want to use too many words! In developing your vision, consider developing a vision that is short enough to become a team cheer of sorts – make it personal.

A team vision (or cheer) consists of only a few words and serves to keep people focused on the *main thing, the main objective*. A well written vision of this type has essential characteristics:

1. It is short and memorable. No one will need to go find a poster on the wall to remember it!
2. It serves to inspire people.
3. A team vision expands current beliefs about what is possible.
4. People have been given the opportunity to buy-in and believe attainment is possible.
5. It unifies employees around a core goal.

The team vision should be meaningful to everyone sharing the work, something that can lift spirits on a tough day, help people refocus when things get crazy, and create unity within the team.

Team Cheer Examples:

"Sixty in six!" – Used by a team that needed to raise sixty thousand dollars in six months to achieve a corporate goal.

"Best in the land!" – Used by a team who was declared the best team in their division. They wanted to remain number one!

One important aspect of this vision, like any vision, is that it can become either ineffective or obsolete at some point. Awesome! That means you have reached a new chapter and it's time to change the team vision! Consider this a sign of success.

EPILOGUE – THE SECRET

I'm often asked,

"What is the secret to becoming a better boss?"

Quite simple really, it's all about your people.

**The job of the boss is to
get the work done through others.**

Those others are your people, your staff.

Treat them well.

Think of them at every turn.

Let them know you care.

Allow them to help you.

Develop them so they can be problem solvers,
not problem makers.

Trust that intentions are good
and they want to do good work.

Appreciate them.

ABOUT THE AUTHOR

Lorna Kibbey is a content speaker who focuses on helping leaders develop their most important, and most complex resources, people! Lorna designs and delivers leadership seminars and motivational keynotes to a variety of audiences in the public and private sector. She is certified to facilitate workplace and team assessments for all levels of employees, using Everything DiSC™, and Five Behaviors of a Cohesive Team™.

Lorna has first-hand experience in dealing with the most difficult situations leaders face. She served as a leader and manager for more than 24 years in the public sector and now works with a wide array of organizations in helping leaders improve performance. While in the public sector, she was recognized as "Best Boss of the Year" in a nationwide initiative!

The topics discussed in these guides are the subject of workshops and keynotes Lorna delivers. If you are interested in bringing Lorna into your organization, please contact her at LKibbey@LKibbey.com.

42775955R00061

Made in the USA
Columbia, SC
23 December 2018